A Tempest

AIMÉ CÉSAIRE

A Tempest

BASED ON SHAKESPEARE'S *THE TEMPEST*
ADAPTATION FOR A BLACK THEATRE

TRANSLATED FROM THE FRENCH
BY RICHARD MILLER

TCG TRANSLATIONS
NEW YORK
2002

A Tempest is published by Theatre Communications Group, Inc.,
520 Eighth Avenue, 24th Floor, New York, NY 10018-4156.

This translation was originally commissioned and published by
the Ubu Repertory Theater.

This publication is made possible in part with public funds from the New York State Council on the Arts, a State Agency.

TCG books are exclusively distributed to the book trade by Consortium Book Sales and Distribution, 1045 Westgate Drive, St. Paul, MN 55114.

Library of Congress Cataloging-in-Publication Data
Césaire, Aimé
[Tempête. English]
A tempest: based on Shakespeare's The tempest : adaptation for a Black theatre / Aimé Césaire ; translated from the French by Richard Miller.
p.cm.
ISBN-13: 978-1-55936-210-8
ISBN-10: 1-55936-210-3 (alk. paper)
I. Miller, Richard. II. Shakespeare, William, 1564–1616. Tempest. III. Title.
PQ3949.C44 T413 2002
822.3'3—dc21   2002007439

Composition by Eliad Design
Cover design and watercolor copyright © 2002 by Barry Moser

First TCG Edition, August 2002
Thirteenth Printing, November 2021

Contents

Poetry & the Political Imagination:
Aimé Césaire, Negritude &
the Applications of Surrealism

(An Introduction)
by Robin D. G. Kelley

vii

A Tempest

I

Poetry & the Political Imagination: Aimé Césaire, Negritude & the Applications of Surrealism

BY ROBIN D. G. KELLEY

Aimé Césaire demolishes the old maxim that poets make terrible politicians. Known in the world of letters as the progenitor of Negritude (the first diasporic "black pride" movement), a major voice of Surrealism, and one of the great French poets, Césaire is equally revered for his role in modern anticolonial and Pan-African movements. While it might appear that the poet and politician operated in separate spheres, Césaire's life and work demonstrate that poetry can be the motor of political imagination, a potent weapon in any movement that claims freedom as its primary goal.

Born on June 25, 1913, in the small town of Basse-Pointe, Martinique, Césaire and his five siblings were raised by their mother, who was a dressmaker, and their father, who held a post as a local tax inspector. Although their father was well educated and they shared the cultural sensibilities of the petite bourgeoisie, the Césaires nonetheless lived close to the edge of rural poverty. Aimé turned out to be a brilliant, precocious student and at age eleven was admitted to the Lycée Schoelcher in Fort-de-France. Upon graduation in 1931, he moved to Paris and enrolled in the Lycée Louis-le-Grand to prepare for the grueling entrance exams to the École Normale Supérieure (a high-level teachers' training college). There he met a number of like-minded intellectuals, most notably the Senegalese intellectual Léopold Sédar Senghor. Among other things, they began to study African history and culture, particularly the writings of German ethnologist Leo Frobenius, whose *Voice of Africa* provided a powerful defense of Africa's cultural and intellectual contributions to the world.

The twosome, along with Césaire's childhood friend, poet Léon-Gontran Damas, launched a journal called *L'Étudiant Noir* (*The Black Student*). In its March 1935 issue, Césaire published a passionate tract against assimilation in which he first coined the term "Negritude." It is more than ironic that at the moment Césaire's piece appeared, he was hard at work absorbing as much knowledge about French and European humanities as possible in preparation for his entrance exams for École Normale Supérieure. The exams took their toll, for sure, though the psychic and emotional costs of having to imbibe the very culture Césaire publicly rejected must have exacerbated an already exhausting regimen. After completing his exams during the summer of 1935, he took a short vacation to Yugoslavia with a fellow student. While visiting the Adriatic coast, Césaire was overcome with memories of home after seeing a small island from a distance. Moved, he stayed up half the night working on a long poem about the Martinique of his youth—the land, the people, the majesty of the place. The next morning when he inquired about the little island, he was told it was called Martinska. A magical chance encounter, to say the least; the words he penned that moonlit night were the beginnings of what would subsequently become his most famous poem of all: *Cahier d'un retour au pays natal* (*Notebook of a Return to My Native Land*).

He did subsequently return to his native land in the early 1940s, shortly after *Cahier* was published, and he was joined by his wife Suzanne Roussy, a fellow Martinican student with whom he had worked on *L'Étudiant Noir*. They both took teaching posts in Fort-de-France and, along with other intellectuals such as René Ménil, Lucie Thésée and Aristide Maugée, launched a journal called *Tropiques* in 1941. Its appearance coincided with the fall of France to the fascist Vichy regime, which consequently put the colonies of Martinique, Guadeloupe and Guiana under Vichy rule and shattered any illusions Césaire and his comrades might have harbored about color-blind French brotherhood. The racism and authoritarianism of the regime was blatant and direct. Vichy officials censored and interdicted all literature they deemed subversive, thus forcing *Tropiques*'s editors to camouflage their publication as a journal of West Indian folklore. Yet, despite the repressions and the ruses, *Tropiques* survived the war as a major voice for Surrealism and a critical forum for the evolution of a sophisticated anticolonial stance as well as a vision of a postcolonial future. The Césaires and their fellow editors promoted a vision of freedom that drew on modernism and a deep appreciation for precolonial African modes of thought and practice; this vision drew on Surrealism as the strategy for revolution of the mind and on Marxism for revolution of the productive forces. It was an effort to carve out a position independent of all these forces—a kind of merging of Negritude, Marxism and Surrealism.

As the essays and poems in *Tropiques* demonstrate, both Césaires contributed profoundly to the development of Surrealist thought and practice. For Aimé Césaire, in particular, Surrealism was an extension of his search for a new black subjectivity, which he had sought in Negritude. "This, for me, was a call to Africa. I said to myself: it's true that superficially we are French, we bear the marks of French customs; we have been branded by Cartesian philosophy, by French rhetoric; but if we break with all that, if we plumb the depths, then what we will find is fundamentally black." Thus throughout the 1940s, he maintained his ties with both Surrealism and Negritude, serving as a founding editor of the journal *Présence Africaine* while continuing to be published in Surrealist publications such as *Le Surrealisme en 1947*, an exhibit catalog edited by André Breton and Marcel Duchamp. Indeed, some of his best known Surrealist works appeared in two poetry collections from that era, *Les Armes Miraculeuses (Miraculous Weapons)* in 1946, *Soleil cou Coupé (Beheaded Sun)* in 1948 and *Corps Perdu (Lost Body)* in 1950, which contained thirty-two engravings by Pablo Picasso.

The end of the war, Césaire became more directly involved in politics, joining the Communist Party and successfully running for mayor of Fort-de-France and deputy to the French National Assembly under the Communist ticket. His main concern, however, was not proletarian revolution but the colonial question. In 1946, he succeeded in getting the National Assembly to pass a law changing the status of Martinique, Guadeloupe, Guiana and Réunion from colonies to "departments" within the French Republic. He believed that the assimilation of the old colonies into the republic would guarantee equal rights, but this turned out not to be the case. In the end, French officials were sent to the colonies in greater numbers, often displacing some of the local black Martinican bureaucrats. It was a painful lesson for Césaire, one that powerfully molded his first and perhaps most important nonfiction book, *Discourse on Colonialism*.

First published in 1950, *Discourse on Colonialism* is indisputably one of the key contributions to a wave of anticolonial literature produced during the postwar period—works that include W. E. B. DuBois's *Color and Democracy* (1945) and *The World of Africa* (1947), Frantz Fanon's *Black Skin, White Masks* (1952), George Padmore's *Pan-Africanism or Communism?: The Coming Struggle for Africa* (1956), Albert Memmi's *The Colonizer and the Colonized* (1957) and Richard Wright's *White Man, Listen!* (1957). As with much of the radical literature produced during this epoch, *Discourse* places the colonial question front and center. In fine Hegelian fashion, Césaire argues that colonialism works to "decivilize" the colonizer: torture, violence, race hatred and immorality constitute a dead weight on the so-called civilized, pulling the master class deeper and deeper into the abyss of barbarism. The instruments of colonial power rely on barbaric, brutal violence and intimidation, and the end result is the degradation of Europe itself. *Discourse*, then, has a double-edged meaning: it is Césaire's discourse on the material and spiritual havoc created by colonialism, and it is also a critique of colonial discourse. Anticipating the explosion of work we now call "postcolonial studies," Césaire reveals how the circulation of colonial ideology—an ideology of racial and cultural hierarchy—is as essential to colonial rule as the police and the use of forced labor. Furthermore, as a product of the post-World War II period, *Discourse* goes one step further by drawing a direct link between the logic of colonialism and the rise of fascism. He provocatively points out that Europeans tolerated "Nazism before it was inflicted on them . . . because, until then, it had been applied only to non-European peoples; that they have cultivated Nazism, that they are responsible for it, and that before engulfing the whole of Western, Christian civilization in its reddened waters, it oozes, seeps and trickles from every crack."

The political implications for Césaire were that colonialism had to be overthrown and a new culture had to replace it, one that embraced non-Western traditions while also embracing the best that modernity had to offer. He outlined this argument in a paper titled "Culture and Colonization," delivered at the First International Congress of Negro Writers and Artists in September 1956. Ultimately, Césaire's insistence that colonialism and racism were the fundamental problems facing the modern world could not be reconciled with the Communist position that promoting proletarian revolution should take precedence over all other struggles. One month later, Césaire penned his famous "Letter to Maurice Thorez, Secretary General of the French Communist Party," tendering his resignation from the party. Arguing that people of color need to exercise self-determination, he warned against treating the "colonial question . . . as a subsidiary part of some more important global matter." Racism, in other words, cannot be subordinate to the class struggle. If following the Communist Party "pillages our most vivifying friendships, wastes the bond that weds us to other West Indian islands, the tie that makes us Africa's child, then I say Communism has served us ill in having us swap a living brotherhood for what looks to have the features of the coldest of all chill abstractions."

Césaire, like his former student Franz Fanon, was now convinced that only Third World revolt could pave the way for a new society. He had practically given up on Europe and the old humanism and its claims of universality, opting instead to redefine the "universal" in a way that did not privilege Europe. "I have a different idea of a universal," Césaire explained to his former Communist comrades. "It is of a universal rich with all that is particular, rich with all the particulars there are, the deepening of each particular, the coexistence of them all."

Césaire went on to found the Martinican Progressive Party and serve as mayor of Fort-de-France for the next two-and-a-half decades, and he continued to write. In 1960, he published *Ferrements*, a collection of forty-eight poems about black liberation and new possibilities created by independence. Using the metaphor of transforming slavery's chains into metal armor, Césaire saw the future of Africa and the diaspora as a phoenix rising. A year later he released *Cadastre*, which included previous poems from *Soleil cou Coupé* and *Corps Perdu*. Whereas Africa was rising (with the exception of places still under white minority rule), Europe here is depicted as a land of petrifaction and rot.

The themes of colonialism and postcolonialism dominated Césaire's work during the 1960s, so much so that he increasingly turned to history in order to explore the problems and prospects of anticolonial revolution. In 1961, he published his second major work of nonfiction: *Toussaint L'Ouverture: La Révolution Française et le Problème Colonial (Toussaint L'Ouverture: The French Revolution and the Problem of Colonialism)*. Césaire tried to show that the French Revolution failed as much as the Haitian Revolution to achieve true liberty. Toussaint not only wanted to destroy slavery on the island of Saint Domingue but wanted to turn these ex-slaves into efficient producers for a world market, to bring his country into the modern world as citizens of the French empire. While the revolution successfully fulfilled the first goal, his dream of a modern Haiti joining a French common-wealth as equal partners was an abysmal failure. That dream died with him in a cold jail cell in Napoleon's France. Unlike other critics, Césaire argued that Toussaint's failure lay not so much in his ambition or his ideas as in his overreliance on the military to solve social, political and economic problems. His critique of Toussaint carried with it a veiled critique of military dictators emerging in postcolonial Africa and Latin America—a critique made explicit in his 1963 play, *La Tragedie du roi Christophe (The Tragedy of King Christophe)*. While grounded in Césaire's reading of Haitian history, it was also a critique of François Duvalier, Haiti's ruler from 1957 through 1971. It explores the many dimensions of post-colonial corruption, depicting Christophe as a deeply flawed but well-meaning tyrant exploiting the black masses trapped on the island. Césaire's next play, *Un Saison au Congo (A Season in the Congo)* (1965), about Patrice Lumumba and the struggle for independence in the Congo, went one step fur-ther, suggesting that only revolution and the violent over-throw of these dictatorships could bring about any real change.

In his final exploration of colonialism, Césaire retreated from modern history and turned to Shakespeare as his vehi-cle. His 1969 adaptation of *The Tempest (Une Tempête)* explored the relationship between Prospero the colonizer and his colonial subjects, Caliban and Ariel. Caliban rebels outright, whereas Ariel attempts to appeal to Prospero's moral conscience. Caliban is eventually crushed when he attempts to become his own master, but not before figuring out that Prospero's domination and claims to superiority are based on lies. Caliban's final speech could have come straight from Césaire's mouth, or the mouths of the radical black intelligentsia produced by colonial education:

> Prospero, you are the master of illusion.
> Lying is your trademark.
> And you have lied so much to me
> (lied about the world, lied about me)
> that you have ended by imposing on me
> an image of myself.
> Underdeveloped, you brand me, inferior,
> that's the way you have forced me to see myself.
> I detest that image! What's more, it's a lie!
> But now I know you, you old cancer,
> and I know myself as well.

During the course of the next three decades, Césaire continued to write but moved away from the epic hero and the problems of the colonial encounter. The Surrealism that had always undergirded his work resurfaced more explicitly in his 1976 collection *Noira* as well as his last play, *Moi, Laminaire* (1982), both of which explored language and reveled in the ambiguous, dreamlike characteristics of the unconscious.

The weapon of poetry may be Césaire's greatest gift to a modern world still searching for freedom. As one of the last truly great "universalists" of the twentieth century, he has had a hand in shaping or critiquing many of the major ideologies and movements of the modern world—Marxism, nationalism, Pan-Africanism and fascism, among others. All of these ideas are rooted in notions of progress, all are products of modernity, and all fall short when it comes to envisioning a genuinely emancipatory future. Césaire must have known this, which is why more than half a century ago he wrote: "Poetic knowledge is born in the great silence of scientific knowledge."

Robin D. G. Kelly teaches history at New York University and is the author of *Yo Mama's Dysfunktional!* (Beacon, 1998) and *Race Rebels: Culture, Politics and the Black Working Class* (Free Press, 1996).

A Tempest

PRODUCTION HISTORY

A Tempest, in Richard Miller's translation, had its American premiere at New York City's Ubu Repertory Theater (Françoise Kourilsky, Artistic Director) on October 9, 1991. The production was directed by Robbie McCauley; set design was by Jane Sablow, lighting design was by Zebedee Collins, costume design was by Carol Ann Pelletier, musical direction was by Tiyé Giraud and movement direction was by Marlies Yearby. The cast was as follows:

ARIEL	Rafael Baez
TRINCULO/CAPTAIN	Ron Brice
CALIBAN	Leon Addison Brown
STEPHANO	Leo V. Finnie, III
GONZALO	Clebert Ford
PROSPERO	Arthur French
GODDESS	Tiyé Giraud
FERDINAND	Bryan Hicks
ALONSO	Lawrence James
ESHU/MASTER OF CEREMONIES	Jasper McGruder
MIRANDA	Sharon McGruder
SEBASTIAN	Patrick Rameau
ANTONIO	Kim Sullivan
GODDESS	Marlies Yearby

CHARACTERS

As in Shakespeare, with:

Two alterations:
ARIEL, a mulatto slave
CALIBAN, a black slave

An addition:
ESHU, a black devil-god

The translation of Amié Césaire's *Une Tempête* presented more challenges than usually arise in the transfer of a play from one language into another (differences in cultural background, tone, milieu and so on). Although Césaire has denied attempting any linguistic echo of Shakespeare, the transposition of his play into English inevitably calls up such echoes, for the literate English/American playgoer cannot help but "hear," behind the language of the play, the original text resounding in all its well-known beauty, its familiarity. For the translator, therefore, the temptation to quote the Ariel songs, for example, or to paraphrase them, was strong. When Césaire has his Ariel sing of something "proche et étrange," for example, Shakespeare's "rich and strange" must, inevitably, sound in the translator's mind.

I have attempted to avoid temptation (there is, if I recall, only one instance of direct quotation in the prose text, but it fell so aptly into place that I was unable to resist); in the main I have left the (slightly altered) song for Ariel with its Shakespearean references unchanged. In an appendix I have now added a "literal" translation of Césaire's text to give a better notion of the imagery he uses for the character. As for the other songs in the text, the options indicated are extremely free adaptations or indications of what I felt to be the substance of the originals or (as in the case of "Oh, Susannah" and "Blow the Man Down") songs familiar to an English-speaking audience that I thought reflected something of the spirit and possible familiarity of the originals.

For this revised edition [1992], I have also included, as an appendix, a "literal" translation of these songs as they occur in French.

Then there is the question of overall tone of voice, taken for granted in *The Tempest*, where social classes, the real and the spirit worlds, are a given. In *A Tempest*, with its Caribbean (and therefore colonial) setting and its consecration to a black theatre, it is essential, I feel, for the director and the actors to decide what accents, what "classes," they wish the various characters to reflect. In my own head, I have heard Ariel's song, for example, as vaguely calypso; others will have other ideas. The director may also wish to emphasize the "political" aspects of the play, in which case the accents employed by the actors would tend to serve that purpose. In any event, in translating the play I have tried not to indicate accent (other than in the Ariel song) and where slang or obscenities have been employed, the emphasis to be given will be set by the director or actor in the way that will best reflect and enhance the tone and style of the particular production.

Prologue

Ambience of a psychodrama. The actors enter singly, at random, and each chooses for himself a mask at his leisure.

MASTER OF CEREMONIES: Come, gentlemen, help yourselves. To each his character, to each character his
mask. You, Prospero? Why not? He has reserves of
willpower he's not even aware of himself. You want
Caliban? Well, that's revealing. Ariel? Fine with me.
And what about Stephano, Trinculo? No takers? Ah,
just in time! It takes all kinds to make a world.

   And after all, they aren't the worst characters. No
problem about the juvenile leads, Miranda and
Ferdinand. You, okay. And there's no problem about
the villains either: you, Antonio; you, Alonso, perfect!
Oh, Christ! I was forgetting the Gods. Eshu will fit you
like a glove. As for the other parts, just take what you
want and work it out among yourselves. But make up
your minds . . . Now, there's one part I have to pick out
myself: you! It's for the part of the Tempest, and I
need a storm to end all storms . . . I need a really big
guy to do the wind. Will you do that? Fine! And then

7

someone strong for Captain of the ship. Good, now let's go. Ready? Begin. Blow, winds! Rain and lightning . . . *ad-lib*!

Act I

GONZALO: Of course, we're only straws tossed on the raging
sea . . . but all's not lost, gentlemen. We just have to try
to get to the eye of the storm.

ANTONIO: We might have known this old fool would nag us
to death!

SEBASTIAN: To the bitter end!

GONZALO: Try to understand what I'm telling you: imagine
a huge cylinder like the chimney of a lamp, fast as a
galloping horse, but in the center as still and unmoving
as Cyclops' eye. That's what we're talking about when
we say "the eye of the storm" and that's where we
have to get.

ANTONIO: Oh, great! Do you really mean that the cyclone or
Cyclops, if he can't see the beam in his own eye, will let
us escape! Oh, that's very illuminating!

GONZALO: It's a clever way of putting it, at any rate.
Literally false, but yet quite true. But what's the fuss
going on up there? The captain seems worried.
(Calling) Captain!

9

CAPTAIN *(With a shrug)*: Boatswain!

BOATSWAIN: Aye, sir!

CAPTAIN: We're coming 'round windward of the island. At this speed we'll run aground. We've got to turn her around. Heave to! *(Exits)*

BOATSWAIN: Come on, men! Heave to! To the topsail: man the ropes. Pull! Heave ho, heave ho!

ALONSO *(Approaching)*: Well, Boatswain, how are things going? Where are we?

BOATSWAIN: If you ask me, you'd all be better off below, in your cabins.

ANTONIO: *He* doesn't seem too happy. We'd better ask the captain. Where's the captain, Boatswain? He was here just a moment ago, and now he's gone off.

BOATSWAIN: Get back below where you belong! We've got work to do!

GONZALO: My dear fellow, I can quite understand your being nervous, but a man should be able to control himself in any situation, even the most upsetting.

BOATSWAIN: Shove it! If you want to save your skins, you'd better get yourselves back down below to those first-class cabins of yours.

GONZALO: Now, now, my good fellow, you don't seem to know to whom you're speaking. *(Making introductions)* The king's brother, the king's son and myself, the king's counselor.

BOATSWAIN: King! King! Well, there's someone who doesn't give a fuck more about the king than he does about you or me, and he's called the Gale. His Majesty the Gale! And right now, he's in control and we're all his subjects.

GONZALO: He might just as well be pilot on the ferry to hell . . . his mouth's foul enough!

ANTONIO: In a sense, the fellow *re*gales me, as you might say. We'll pull through, you'll see, because he looks to me more like someone who'll end up on the gallows, not beneath the billows.

SEBASTIAN: The end result is the same. The fish will get us and the crows will get him.

GONZALO: He did irritate me, rather. However, I take the attenuating circumstances into account . . . and, you must admit, he lacks neither courage nor wit.

BOATSWAIN *(Returning)*: Pull in the stud sails. Helmsman, into the wind! Into the wind!

(Noticing Sebastian, Antonio, Gonzalo) You again! If you keep bothering us and don't get below and say your prayers I'll give up and let you sail the ship! You can't expect me to be the go-between for your souls and Beelzebub!

ANTONIO: It's really too much! The fellow is taking advantage of the situation . . .

BOATSWAIN: Windward! Windward! Heave into the wind!

(Thunder, lightning.)

SEBASTIAN: Ho! Ho!

GONZALO: Did you see that? There, at the top of the masts, in the rigging, that glitter of blue fire, flashing, flashing? They're right when they call these magic lands, so different from our homes in Europe . . . Look, even the lightning is different!

ANTONIO: Maybe it's a foretaste of the hell that awaits us.

GONZALO: You're too pessimistic. Anyway, I've always kept myself in a state of grace, ready to meet my maker.

(Enter sailors.)

SAILORS: Shit! We're sinking!

(The passengers can be heard singing "Nearer, My God, to Thee.")

BOATSWAIN: To leeward! To leeward!

FERDINAND *(Entering)*: Alas! There's no one in hell . . . all the devils are here!

(The ship sinks.)

SCENE 2

MIRANDA: Oh God! Oh God! A sinking ship! Father, help!

(Enter Prospero, hurriedly carrying a megaphone.)

PROSPERO: Come, Daughter, calm yourself! It's only a play. There's really nothing wrong. Anyway, everything that happens is for our own good. Trust me, I won't say any more.

MIRANDA: But such a fine ship, and so many fine, brave lives sunk, drowned, laid waste to wrack and ruin . . . A person would have to have a heart of stone not to be moved . . .

PROSPERO: Drowned . . . hmmm. That remains to be seen. But draw near, dear princess. The time has come.

MIRANDA: You're making fun of me, Father. Wild as I am, you know I am happy—like a queen of the wildflowers, of streams and paths, running barefoot through thorns and flowers, spared by one, caressed by the other.

PROSPERO: But you are a princess . . . for how else does one
   address the daughter of a prince? I cannot leave you in
   ignorance any longer. Milan is the city of your birth,
   and the city where for many years I was the duke.

MIRANDA: Then how did we come here? And tell me, too, by
   what ill fortune did a prince turn into the reclusive her-
   mit you are now, here, on this desert isle? Was it
   because you found the world distasteful, or through the
   perfidy of some enemy? Is our island a prison or a her-
   mitage? You've hinted at some mystery so many times
   and aroused my curiosity, and today you shall tell
   me all.

PROSPERO: In a way, it is because of all the things you mention. First, it is because of political disagreements,
   because of the intrigues of my ambitious younger
   brother. Antonio is his name, your uncle, and Alonso
   the name of the envious King of Naples. How their
   ambitions were joined, how my brother became the
   accomplice of my rival, how the latter promised the
   former his protection and my throne . . . the devil alone
   knows how all that came about. In any event, when they
   learned that through my studies and experiments I had
   managed to discover the exact location of these lands
   for which many had sought for centuries and that I was
   making preparations to set forth to take possession of
   them, they hatched a scheme to steal my as-yet-unborn
   empire from me. They bribed my people, they stole my
   charts and documents and, to get rid of me, they
   denounced me to the Inquisition as a magician and sorcerer. To be brief, one day I saw arriving at the palace
   men to whom I had never granted audience: the Priests
   of the Holy Office.

(Flashback: Standing before Prospero, who is wearing his ducal robes, we see a friar reading from a parchment scroll.)

THE FRIAR: The Holy Inquisition for the preservation and integrity of the Faith and the pursuit of heretical perversion, acting through the special powers entrusted to it by the Holy Apostolic See, informed of the errors you profess, insinuate and publish against God and his Creation with regard to the shape of the Earth, and the possibility of discovering other lands, notwithstanding the fact that the Prophet Isaiah stated and taught that the Lord God is seated upon the circle of the Earth and in its center is Jerusalem and that around the world lies inaccessible Paradise, convinced that it is through wickedness that to support your heresy you quote Strabus, Ptolemy and the tragic author Seneca, thereby lending credence to the notion that profane writings can aspire to an authority equal to that of the most profound of the Holy Scriptures, given your notorious use by both night and day of Arabic calculations and scribblings in Hebrew, Syrian and other demonic tongues and, lastly, given that you have hitherto escaped punishment owing to your temporal authority and have, if not usurped, then transformed that authority and made it into a tyranny, doth hereby strip you of your titles, positions and honors in order that it may then proceed against you according to due process through a full and thorough examination, under which authority we require that you accompany us.

PROSPERO *(Back in the present)*: And yet, the trial they said they were going to hold never took place. Such creatures of darkness are too much afraid of the light.

To be brief: instead of killing me they chose—even worse—to maroon me here with you on this desert island.

MIRANDA: How terrible, and how wicked the world is! How you must have suffered!

PROSPERO: In all this tale of treason and felony there is but one honorable name: Gonzalo, the counselor to the King of Naples and fit to serve a better master. By furnishing me with food and clothing, by supplying me with my books and instruments, he has done all in his power to make my exile in this disgusting place bearable. And now, through a singular turn, Fortune has brought to these shores the very men involved in the plot against me. My prophetic science had of course already informed me that they would not be content merely with seizing my lands in Europe and that their greed would win out over their cowardice, that they would confront the sea and set out for those lands my genius had discovered. I couldn't let them get away with that, and since I was able to stop them, I did so, with the help of Ariel. We brewed up the storm you have just witnessed, thereby saving my possessions overseas and bringing the scoundrels into my power at the same time.

(Enter Ariel.)

Well, Ariel?

ARIEL: Mission accomplished.

PROSPERO: Bravo; good work! But what seems to be the matter? I give you a compliment and you don't seem pleased? Are you tired?

ARIEL: Not tired; disgusted. I obeyed you but—well, why not come out with it? I did so most unwillingly. It was a real pity to see that great ship go down, so full of life.

PROSPERO: Oh, so you're upset, are you! It's always like that with you intellectuals! Who cares! What interests me is not your moods, but your deeds. Let's split: I'll take the zeal and you can keep your doubts. Agreed?

ARIEL: Master, I must beg you to spare me this kind of labor.

PROSPERO *(Shouting)*: Listen, and listen good! There's a task to be performed, and I don't care how it gets done!

ARIEL: You've promised me my freedom a thousand times, and I'm still waiting.

PROSPERO: Ingrate! And who freed you from Sycorax, may I ask? Who rent the pine in which you had been imprisoned and brought you forth?

ARIEL: Sometimes I almost regret it . . . After all, I might have turned into a real tree in the end . . . Tree: that's a word that really gives me a thrill! It often springs to mind: palm tree—springing into the sky like a fountain ending in nonchalant, squid-like elegance. The baobab—twisted like the soft entrails of some monster. Ask the calao bird that lives a cloistered season in its branches. Or the ceiba tree—spread out beneath the proud sun. O bird, O green mansions set in the living earth!

PROSPERO: Stuff it! I don't like talking trees. As for your freedom, you'll have it when I'm good and ready. In the meanwhile, see to the ship. I'm going to have a few words with Master Caliban. I've been keeping my eye on him, and he's getting a little too emancipated. *(Exit Ariel)*
   (Calling) Caliban! Caliban! *(He sighs)*

(Enter Caliban.)

CALIBAN: Uhuru!

PROSPERO: What did you say?

CALIBAN: I said, Uhuru!

PROSPERO: Mumbling your native language again! I've already told you, I don't like it. You could be polite, at least; a simple "hello" wouldn't kill you.

CALIBAN: Oh, I forgot . . . But make that as froggy, waspish, pustular and a dung-filled "hello" as possible. May today hasten by a decade the day when all the birds of the sky and beasts of the earth will feast upon your corpse!

PROSPERO: Gracious as always, you ugly ape! How can anyone be so ugly?

CALIBAN: You think I'm ugly . . . well, I don't think you're so handsome yourself. With that big hooked nose, you look just like some old vulture. *(Laughing)* An old vulture with a scrawny neck!

PROSPERO: Since you're so fond of invective, you could at least thank me for having taught you to speak at all. You, a savage . . . a dumb animal, a beast I educated, trained, dragged up from the bestiality that still clings to you.

CALIBAN: In the first place, that's not true. You didn't teach me a thing! Except to jabber in your own language so that I could understand your orders: chop the wood, wash the dishes, fish for food, plant vegetables, all because you're too lazy to do it yourself. And as for your learning, did you ever impart any of *that* to me? No, you took care not to. All your science you keep for yourself alone, shut up in those big books.

PROSPERO: What would you be without me?

CALIBAN: Without you? I'd be the king, that's what I'd be, the King of the Island. The King of the Island given me by my mother, Sycorax.

PROSPERO: There are some family trees it's better not to climb! She's a ghoul! A witch from whom—and may God be praised—death has delivered us.

CALIBAN: Dead or alive, she was my mother, and I won't deny her! Anyhow, you only think she's dead because you think the earth itself is dead . . . It's so much simpler that way! Dead, you can walk on it, pollute it, you can tread upon it with the steps of a conqueror. I respect the earth, because I know that Sycorax is alive.

> Sycorax. Mother.
> Serpent, rain, lightning.
> And I see thee everywhere!
> In the eye of the stagnant pool which stares back at me,
> through the rushes,
> in the gesture made by twisted root and its awaiting thrust.
> In the night, the all-seeing blinded night,
> the nostril-less all-smelling night!

. . . Often, in my dreams, she speaks to me and warns me . . . Yesterday, even, when I was lying by the stream on my belly lapping at the muddy water, when the Beast was about to spring upon me with that huge stone in his hand . . .

PROSPERO: If you keep on like that even your magic won't save you from punishment!

CALIBAN: That's right, that's right! In the beginning, the gentleman was all sweet talk: dear Caliban here, my little Caliban there! And what do you think you'd have done without me in this strange land? Ingrate! I taught you the trees, fruits, birds, the seasons, and now you don't give a damn . . . Caliban the animal, Caliban the slave! I know that story! Once you've squeezed the juice from the orange, you toss the rind away!

PROSPERO: Oh!

CALIBAN: Do I lie? Isn't it true that you threw me out of your house and made me live in a filthy cave. The ghetto!

PROSPERO: It's easy to say "ghetto"! It wouldn't be such a ghetto if you took the trouble to keep it clean! And there's something you forgot, which is that what forced me to get rid of you was your lust. Good God, you tried to rape my daughter!

CALIBAN: Rape! Rape! Listen, you old goat, you're the one that put those dirty thoughts in my head. Let me tell you something: I couldn't care less about your daughter, or about your cave, for that matter. If I gripe, it's on principle, because I didn't like living with you at all, as a matter of fact. Your feet stink!

PROSPERO: I did not summon you here to argue. Out! Back to work! Wood, water, and lots of both! I'm expecting company today.

CALIBAN: I've had just about enough. There's already a pile of wood that high . . .

PROSPERO: Enough! Careful, Caliban! If you keep grumbling you'll be whipped. And if you don't step lively, if you keep dragging your feet or try to strike or sabotage things, I'll beat you. Beating is the only language you really understand. So much the worse for you: I'll speak it, loud and clear. Get a move on!

CALIBAN: All right, I'm going . . . but this is the last time. It's the last time, do you hear me? Oh . . . I forgot. I've got something important to tell you.

PROSPERO: Important? Well, out with it.

CALIBAN: It's this: I've decided I don't want to be called Caliban any longer.

PROSPERO: What kind of rot is that? I don't understand.

CALIBAN: Put it this way: I'm *telling* you that from now on I won't answer to the name Caliban.

PROSPERO: Where did you get that idea?

CALIBAN: Well, because Caliban *isn't* my name. It's as simple as that.

PROSPERO: Oh, I suppose it's mine!

CALIBAN: It's the name given me by your hatred, and every time it's spoken it's an insult.

PROSPERO: My, aren't we getting sensitive! All right, suggest something else . . . I've got to call you something. What will it be? Cannibal would suit you, but I'm sure you wouldn't like that, would you? Let's see . . . what about Hannibal? That fits. And why not . . . they all seem to like historical names.

CALIBAN: Call me X. That would be best. Like a man without a name. Or, to be more precise, a man whose name has been stolen. You talk about history . . . well, that's history, and everyone knows it! Every time you summon me it reminds me of a basic fact, the fact that you've stolen everything from me, even my identity! Uhuru! *(He exits)*

(Enter Ariel as a sea-nymph.)

PROSPERO: My dear Ariel, did you see how he looked at me, that glint in his eye? That's something new. Well, let me tell you, Caliban is the enemy. As for those people on the boat, I've changed my mind about them. Give them a scare, but for God's sake don't touch a hair on their heads! You'll answer to me if you do.

ARIEL: I've suffered too much myself for having made them suffer not to be pleased at your mercy. You can count on me, Master.

PROSPERO: Yes, however great their crimes, if they repent you can assure them of my forgiveness. They are men of my race, and of high rank. As for me, at my age one must rise above disputes and quarrels and think about the future. I have a daughter. Alonso has a son. If they were to fall in love, I would give my consent. Let Ferdinand marry Miranda, and may their marriage bring us harmony and peace. That is my plan. I want it executed. As for Caliban, does it matter what the villain plots against me? All the nobility of Italy, Naples and Milan henceforth combined, will protect me. Go!

ARIEL: Yes, Master. Your orders will be fully carried out.

(Exit Prospero.
* Ariel sings:)*

  Sandy seashore, deep blue sky,
  surf is rising, sea birds fly
  here the lover finds delight,
  sun at noontime, moon at night.
  Join hands lovers, join the dance,
  find contentment, find romance.

  Sandy seashore, deep blue sky,
  cares will vanish . . . so can I . . .

(Enter Ferdinand.)

FERDINAND: What is this music? It has led me here and now it stops . . . No, there it is again . . .

ARIEL *(Singing)*:

> Waters move, the ocean flows,
> nothing comes and nothing goes . . .
> Strange days are upon us . . .
>
> Oysters stare through pearly eyes
> heart-shaped corals gently beat
> in the crystal undersea . . .
>
> Waters move and ocean flows
> nothing comes and nothing goes . . .
> Strange days are upon us . . .

FERDINAND: What is this that I see before me? A goddess? A mortal?

MIRANDA: I know what *I'm* seeing: a flatterer. Young man, your ability to pay compliments in the situation in which you find yourself at least proves your courage. Who are you?

FERDINAND: As you see, a poor shipwrecked soul.

MIRANDA: But one of high degree!

FERDINAND: In other surroundings I might be called "Prince," "Son of the King . . ." But, no, I was forgetting . . . not "Prince" but "King," alas . . . "King" because my father has just perished in the shipwreck.

MIRANDA: Poor young man! Here, you'll be received with hospitality and we'll support you in your misfortune.

FERDINAND: Alas, my father . . . Can it be that I am an unnatural son? Your pity would make the greatest of sorrows seem sweet.

MIRANDA: I hope you'll like it here with us. The island is
pretty. I'll show you the beaches and the forests, I'll tell
you the names of the fruits and flowers, I'll introduce
you to a whole world of insects, of lizards of every hue,
of birds . . . Oh, you cannot imagine! The birds! . . .

(Enter Prospero.)

PROSPERO: That's enough, Daughter! I find your chatter
irritating . . . and let me assure you, it's not at all fit-
ting. You are doing too much honor to an impostor.
Young man, you are a traitor, a spy and a woman-chaser
to boot! No sooner has he escaped the perils of the sea
than he's sweet-talking the first girl he meets! You
won't get 'round me that way. Your arrival is conven-
ient, because I need more manpower: you shall be my
house servant.

FERDINAND: Seeing the young lady, more beautiful than any
wood-nymph, I might have been Ulysses on Nausicaa's
isle. But hearing you, sir, I now understand my fate a
little better . . . I see I have come ashore on the Barbary
Coast and am in the hands of a cruel pirate. *(Drawing
his sword)* However, a gentleman prefers death to dis-
honor! I shall defend my life with my freedom!

PROSPERO: Poor fool: your arm is growing weak, your knees
are trembling! Traitor! I could kill you now . . . but
I need the manpower. Follow me.

ARIEL: It's no use trying to resist, young man. My master is
a sorcerer: neither your passion nor your youth can
prevail against him. Your best course would be to follow and obey him.

FERDINAND: Oh God! What sorcery is this? Vanquished, a captive—yet far from rebelling against my fate, I am finding my servitude sweet. Oh, I would be imprisoned for life if only heaven will grant me a glimpse of my sun each day, the face of my own sun. Farewell, Nausicaa.

(They exit.)

Act II

SCENE 1

Caliban's cave. Caliban is singing as he works. Ariel enters and listens to him for a moment.

CALIBAN *(Singing)*:

> May he who eats his corn heedless of Shango
> be accursed! May Shango creep beneath
> his nails and eat into his flesh!
> Shango, Shango ho!
>
> Forget to give him room if you dare!
> He will make himself at home on your nose!
>
> Refuse to have him under your roof at your
> own risk!
> He'll tear off your roof and wear it as a hat!
> Whoever tries to mislead Shango
> will suffer for it!
> Shango, Shango ho!

ARIEL: Greetings, Caliban. I know you don't think much of
me, but after all we *are* brothers, brothers in suffering
and slavery, but brothers in hope as well. We both want
our freedom. We just have different methods.

CALIBAN: Greetings to you. But you didn't come to see me
just to make that profession of faith. Come on, Alastor!
The old man sent you, didn't he? A great job: carrying
out the Master's fine ideas, his great plans.

ARIEL: No, I've come on my own. I came to warn you.
Prospero is planning horrible acts of revenge against
you. I thought it my duty to alert you.

CALIBAN: I'm ready for him.

ARIEL: Poor Caliban, you're doomed. You know that you
aren't the stronger, you'll never be the stronger. What
good will it do you to struggle?

CALIBAN: And what about you? What good has your obedi-
ence done you, your Uncle Tom patience and your
sucking up to him. The man's just getting more
demanding and despotic day by day.

ARIEL: Well, I've at least achieved one thing: he's promised
me my freedom. In the distant future, of course, but
it's the first time he's actually committed himself.

CALIBAN: Talk's cheap! He'll promise you a thousand times
and take it back a thousand times. Anyway, tomorrow
doesn't interest me. What I want is *(Shouting)* Freedom Now!

ARIEL: Okay. But you know you're not going to get it out
of him "now," and that he's stronger than you are. I'm
in a good position to know just what he's got in his
arsenal.

CALIBAN: The stronger? How do you know that? Weakness
always has a thousand ways and cowardice is all that
keeps us from listing them.

ARIEL: I don't believe in violence.

CALIBAN: What *do* you believe in, then? In cowardice? In
giving up? In kneeling and groveling? That's it, someone strikes you on the right cheek and you offer the
left. Someone kicks you on the left buttock and you
turn the right . . . that way there's no jealousy. Well,
that's not Caliban's way . . .

ARIEL: You know very well that's not what I mean. No violence, no submission either. Listen to me: Prospero is
the one we've got to change. Destroy his serenity so
that he's finally forced to acknowledge his own injustice
and put an end to it.

CALIBAN: Oh sure . . . that's a good one! Prospero's conscience!
Prospero is an old scoundrel who has no conscience.

ARIEL: Exactly—that's why it's up to us to give him one. I'm
not fighting just for *my* freedom, for *our* freedom, but
for Prospero too, so that Prospero can acquire a conscience. Help me, Caliban.

CALIBAN: Listen, kid, sometimes I wonder if you aren't a little bit nuts. So that Prospero can acquire a conscience?
You might as well ask a stone to grow flowers.

ARIEL: I don't know what to do with you. I've often had this
inspiring, uplifting dream that one day Prospero, you,
me, we would all three set out, like brothers, to build a
wonderful world, each one contributing his own special
thing: patience, vitality, love, willpower too, and rigor,
not to mention the dreams without which mankind
would perish.

CALIBAN: You don't understand a thing about Prospero.
He's not the collaborating type. He's a guy who only
feels something when he's wiped someone out.
A crusher, a pulverizer, that's what he is! And you talk
about brotherhood!

ARIEL: So then what's left? War? And you know that when it comes to that, Prospero is invincible.

CALIBAN: Better death than humiliation and injustice. Anyhow, I'm going to have the last word. Unless nothingness has it. The day when I begin to feel that everything's lost, just let me get hold of a few barrels of your infernal powder and as you fly around up there in your blue skies you'll see this island, my inheritance, my work, all blown to smithereens . . . and, I trust, Prospero and me with it. I hope you'll like the fireworks display—it'll be signed Caliban.

ARIEL: Each of us marches to his own drum. You follow yours. I follow the beat of mine. I wish you courage, brother.

CALIBAN: Farewell, Ariel, my brother, and good luck.

SCENE 2

GONZALO: A magnificent country! Bread hangs from the trees and the apricots are bigger than a woman's full breast.

SEBASTIAN: A pity that it's so wild and uncultivated . . . here and there.

GONZALO: Oh, that's nothing. If there were anything poisonous, an antidote would never be far away, for nature is intrinsically harmonious. I've even read somewhere that guano is excellent compost for sterile ground.

SEBASTIAN: Guano? What kind of animal is that? Are you sure you don't mean iguana?

GONZALO: Young man, if I say guano, I mean guano. Guano is the name for bird droppings that build up over centuries, and it is by far the best fertilizer known. You dig it out of caves . . . if you want my opinion, I think we should investigate all the caves on this island one by one to see if we find any, and if we do, this island, if wisely exploited, will be richer than Egypt with its Nile.

ANTONIO: Let me understand: your guano cave contains a river of dried bird shit.

GONZALO: To pick up on your image, all we need to do is channel that river, use it to irrigate, if I may use the term, the fields with this wonderful fecal matter, and everything will bloom.

SEBASTIAN: But we'll still need manpower to farm it. Is the island even inhabited?

GONZALO: That's the problem, of course. But if it is, it must be by wonderful people. It's obvious: a wondrous land can only contain wonderful creatures.

ANTONIO: Yes!

> Men whose bodies are wiry and strong
> and women whose eyes are open and frank . . .
> creatures in it! . . .

GONZALO: Something like that! I see you know your literature. But in that case, watch out: it will mean new responsibilities for us!

SEBASTIAN: How do you get that?

GONZALO: I mean that if the island is inhabited, as I believe, and if we colonize it, as is my hope, then we have to take every precaution not to import our shortcomings, yes, what we call civilization. They must stay as they are: savages, noble and good savages, free, without any complexes or complications. Something like a pool

granting eternal youth where we periodically come to
restore our aging, citified souls.

ANTONIO: Sir Gonzalo, when will you shut up?

GONZALO: Ah, Your Majesty, if I am boring you, I apologize.
I was only speaking as I did to distract you and to turn
all our sad thoughts to something more pleasant.
There, I'll be silent. Indeed, these old bones have had
it. Oof! Let me sit down . . . with your permission, of
course.

ALONSO: Noble Old Man, even though younger than you,
we are all in the same fix.

GONZALO: In other words, dead tired and dying of hunger.

ALONSO: I have never pretended to be above the human
condition.

(A strange, solemn music is heard.)

. . . Listen, listen! Did you hear that?

GONZALO: Yes, it's an odd melody!

*(Enter Prospero with Ariel, both invisible. Other strange
figures enter as well, bearing a laden table. They dance and
graciously invite the king and his company to eat, then the
creatures disappear.)*

ALONSO: Heaven protect us! Live marionettes!

GONZALO: Such grace! Such music! Hum. The whole thing
is most peculiar.

SEBASTIAN: Gone! Faded away! But what does that matter,
since they've left their food behind! No meal was ever
more welcome. Gentlemen, to table!

ALONSO: Yes, let us partake of this feast, even though it may
be our last.

(They prepare to eat, but elves enter and, with much grimacing and many contortions, carry off the table.)

GONZALO: Ah! That's a fine way to behave!

ALONSO: I have the distinct feeling that we have fallen under the sway of Powers that are playing cat and mouse with us. It's a cruel way to make us aware of our dependent status.

GONZALO: The way things have been going it's not surprising, and it will do us no good to protest.

(The elves return, bringing the food with them.)

ALONSO: Oh no, this time I won't bite!

SEBASTIAN: I'm so hungry that I don't care, I'll abandon my scruples.

GONZALO *(To Alonso)*: Why not try? Perhaps the Powers controlling us saw how disappointed we were and took pity on us. After all, even though disappointed a hundred times, Tantalus still tried a hundred times.

ALONSO: That was also his torture. I won't touch that food.

PROSPERO *(Invisible)*: Ariel, I don't like his refusing. Harass them until they eat.

ARIEL *(Invisible)*: Why should we go to any trouble for them? If they won't eat, they can die of hunger.

PROSPERO: No, I *want* them to eat.

ARIEL: That's despotism. A while ago you made me snatch it away just when they were about to gobble it up, and now that they don't want it you are ready to force feed them.

PROSPERO: Enough hairsplitting! My mood has changed! They insult me by not eating. They must be made to eat out of my hand like chicks. That is a sign of submission I insist they give me.

ARIEL: It's evil to play with their hunger as you do with their
    anxieties and their hopes.
PROSPERO: That is how power is measured. I am Power.

(Alonso and his group eat.)

ALONSO: Alas, when I think . . .
GONZALO: That's your trouble, sire: you think too much.
ALONSO: And thus I should not even think of my lost son!
    My throne! My country!
GONZALO *(Eating)*: Your son! What's to say we won't find
    him again! As for the rest of it . . . Look, sire, this filthy
    hole is now our entire world. Why seek further? If your
    thoughts are too vast, cut them down to size.

(They eat.)

ALONSO: So be it! But I would prefer to sleep. To sleep and
    to forget.
GONZALO: Good idea! Let's put up our hammocks!

(They sleep.)

SCENE 3

Enter Antonio and Sebastian upon the group.

ANTONIO: Look at those leeches, those slugs! Wallowing in
    their slime and their snot: idiots, slime—they're like
    beached jellyfish.

SEBASTIAN: Shhh! It's the king. And that old graybeard is
    his venerable counselor.

ANTONIO: The king is he who watches over his flock when
    they sleep. That one isn't watching over anything.
    Ergo, he's not the king. *(Brusquely)* You're a really
    bloodless lily-liver if you can see a king asleep without
    getting certain ideas . . .

SEBASTIAN: I mustn't have any blood, only water.

ANTONIO: Don't insult water. Every time I look at myself
    I think I'm more handsome, more *there*. My inner
    juices have always given me my greatness, my true
    greatness . . . not the greatness men grant me.

SEBASTIAN: All right, so I'm stagnant water.

ANTONIO: Water is never stagnant. It works, it works in us.
    It is what gives man his dimension, his true one.
    Believe me, you're mistaken if you don't grab the
    opportunity when it's offered you. It may never come
    again.

SEBASTIAN: What are you getting at? I have a feeling I can
    guess.

ANTONIO: Guess, guess! Look at that tree swaying in the
    wind, It's called a coconut palm. My dear Sebastian, in
    my opinion it's time to shake the coconut palm.

SEBASTIAN: Now I really don't understand.

ANTONIO: What a dope! Consider my position: I'm Duke of
    Milan. Well, I wasn't always . . . I had an older brother.
    That was Duke Prospero. And if I'm now Duke Antonio,
    it's because I knew when to shake the coconut palm.

SEBASTIAN: And Prospero?

ANTONIO: What do you mean by that? When you shake a
    tree, someone is bound to fall. And obviously it wasn't
    me who fell, because here I am: to assist and serve you,
    Majesty!

SEBASTIAN: Enough! He's my brother! My scruples won't allow me to . . . You take care of him while I deal with the old counselor.

(They draw their swords.)

ARIEL: Stop, ruffians! Resistance is futile: your swords are enchanted and falling from your hands!

ANTONIO AND SEBASTIAN: Alas! Alas!

ARIEL: Sleepers, awake! Awake, I say! Your life depends on it. With these fine fellows with their long teeth and swords around, anyone who sleeps too soundly risks sleeping forever.

(Alonso and Gonzalo awaken.)

ALONSO *(Rubbing his eyes)*: What's happening? I was asleep, and I was having a terrible dream!

ARIEL: No, you were not dreaming. These fine lords here are criminals who were about to perpetrate the most odious of crimes upon you. Yes, Alonso, you may well marvel that a god should fly to your aid. Were to heaven you deserved it more!

ALONSO: I have never been wanting in respect for the divinity . . .

ARIEL: I don't know what effect my next piece of news will have on you: the name of him who has sent me to you is Prospero.

ALONSO: Prospero! God save us! *(Falls to his knees)*

ARIEL: I understand your feelings. He lives. It is he who reigns over this isle, as he reigns over the spirits of the air you breathe . . . But rise . . . you need fear no longer. He has not saved your lives to destroy them. Your repentance will suffice, for I can see that it is deep and sincere. *(To Antonio and Sebastian)* As for you, gentlemen, my master's pardon extends to you as well, on the condition that you renounce your plans, knowing them to be in vain.

SEBASTIAN *(To Antonio)*: We could have got worse!

ANTONIO: If it were men we were up against, no one could make me withdraw, but when it's demons and magic there's no shame in giving in. *(To Ariel)* . . . We are the duke's most humble and obedient servants. Please beg him to accept our thanks.

GONZALO: Oh, how ignoble! How good of you to just wipe the slate clean! No surface repentance . . . not only do you want attrition, you want contrition as well! Why look at me as though you didn't know what I was talking about? *Attrition*: a selfish regret for offending God, caused by a fear of punishment. *Contrition*: an unselfish regret growing out of sorrow at displeasing God.

ARIEL: Honest Gonzalo, thank you for your clarification. Your eloquence has eased my mission and your pedagogical skill has abbreviated it, for in a few short words you have expressed my master's thought. May your words be heard! Therefore, let us turn the page. To terminate this episode, I need only convoke you all, on my master's behalf, to the celebrations that this very day will mark the engagement of his daughter, Miranda. Alonso, that's good news for you . . .

ALONSO: What—my son?

ARIEL: Correct. Saved by my master from the fury of the waves.

ALONSO *(Falling to his knees)*: God be praised for this blessing more than all the rest. Rank, fortune, throne, I am prepared to forgo all if my son is returned to me . . .

ARIEL: Come, gentlemen, follow me.

Act III

SCENE 1

FERDINAND *(Hoeing and singing)*:

> How life has changed
> now, hoe in hand
> I work away all day . . .
>
> Hoeing all the day,
> I go my weary way . . .

CALIBAN: Poor kid! What would he say if he was Caliban!
He works night and day, and when he sings, it's:

> Oo-en-day, Oo-en-day, Oo-en-day, Macaya . . .

And no pretty girl to console him! *(Sees Miranda
approaching)* Aha! Let's listen to this!

FERDINAND *(Singing)*:

> How my life has changed
> now, hoe in hand
> I work away all day . . .

(Enter Miranda.)

MIRANDA: Poor young man! Can I help you? You don't look like you were cut out for this kind of work!

FERDINAND: One word from you would be more help to me than anything in the world.

MIRANDA: One word? From me? I must say, I . . .

FERDINAND: Your name—that's all: what is your name?

MIRANDA: That, I cannot say! It's impossible. My father has expressly forbidden it!

FERDINAND: It is the only thing I long for.

MIRANDA: But I can't, I tell you; it's forbidden!

CALIBAN *(Taking advantage of Miranda's momentary distraction, he whispers her name to Ferdinand)*: Mi-ran-da!

FERDINAND: All right then, I shall christen you with a name of my own. I will call you Miranda.

MIRANDA: That's too much! What a low trick! You must have heard my father calling me . . . Unless it was that awful Caliban who keeps pursuing me and calling out my name in his stupid dreams!

FERDINAND: No, Miranda . . . I had only to allow my eyes to speak, as you your face.

MIRANDA: Sssh! My father's coming! He'd better not catch you trying to sweet talk me . . .

FERDINAND *(Goes back to work, singing)*:

But times have changed
now, hoeing all the day,
I go my weary way . . .

PROSPERO: That's fine, young man! You've managed to accomplish a good deal for a beginning! I see I've misjudged you. But you won't be the loser if you serve me well. Listen, my young friend, there are three things in life: Work, Patience, Continence, and the world is yours . . . Hey, Caliban, I'm taking this boy away with me. He's done enough for one day. But since the job is urgent, see that it gets finished.

CALIBAN: Me?

PROSPERO: Yes, you! You've cheated me enough with your loafing and fiddling around, so you can work a double shift for once!

CALIBAN: I don't see why I should do someone else's job!

PROSPERO: Who's the boss here? You or me? Listen, monster: if you don't like work, I'll see to it you change your mind!

(Prospero and Ferdinand move away.)

CALIBAN: Go on, go on . . . I'll get you one day, you bastard! *(He sets to work, singing:)*

Oo-en-day, Oo-en-day, Oo-en-day, Macaya . . .

Shit, now it's raining! As if things weren't bad enough . . . *(Suddenly, at the sound of a voice, Caliban stiffens)* Do you hear that, boy? That voice through the storm. Bah! It's Ariel. No, that's not his voice. Whose, then?

With an old coot like Prospero . . . One of his cops,
probably. Oh, fine! Now, I'm for it. Men and the ele-
ments both against me. Well, the hell with it . . . I'm
used to it. Patience! I'll get them yet. In the meantime
better make myself scarce! Let Prospero and his storm
and his cops go by . . . let the seven maws of
Malediction bay!

SCENE 2

Enter Trinculo.

TRINCULO *(Singing)*:

Oh, Susannah . . . oh don't you cry for me . . . *(Etc.)*

You can say that again! My dearest Susannah . . . trust
Trinculo, we've had all the roaring storms we need, and
more! I swear: the whole crew wiped out, liquidated . . .
Nothing! Nothing left! . . . Nothing but poor wander-
ing and wailing Trinculo! No question about it, it'll be
a while before anyone persuades me to depart from
affectionate women and friendly towns to go off to
brave roaring storms! How it's raining! *(Notices Caliban
underneath the wheelbarrow)* Ah, an Indian! Dead or
alive? You never know with these tricky races. Yukkk!
Anyhow, this will do me fine. If he's dead, I can use his
clothes for shelter, for a coat, a tent, a covering. If he's
alive I'll make him my prisoner and take him back to
Europe and then, by golly, my fortune will be made! I'll

sell him to a carnival. No! I'll show him myself at fairs!
What a stroke of luck! I'll just settle in here where it's
warm and let the storm rage!

*(He crawls under cover, back to back with Caliban.
Enter Stephano.)*

STEPHANO *(Singing)*:

> Blow the man down, hearties,
> blow the man down . . . *(Etc.)*

(Takes a swig of his bottle and continues:)

> Blow, blow, blow the man down . . . *(Etc.)*

Fortunately, there's still a little wine left in this bottle . . .
enough to give me courage! Be of good cheer,
Stephano, where there's life there's thirst . . . and vice
versa! *(Suddenly spies Caliban's head sticking out of the
covers)* My God, on Stephano's word, it looks like a
Nindian! *(Comes nearer)* And that's just what it is! A
Nindian. That's neat. I really am lucky. There's money
to be made from a Nindian like that. If you showed
him at a carnival . . . along with the bearded lady and
the flea circus, a real Nindian! An authentic Nindian
from the Caribbean! That means real dough, or I'm the
last of the idiots! *(Touching Caliban)* But he's ice cold!
I don't know what the body temperature of a Nindian
is, but this one seems pretty cold to me! Let's hope he's
not going to croak! How's that for bad luck: you find a
Nindian and he dies on you! A fortune slips through
your fingers! But wait, I've got an idea . . . a good swig

of this booze between his lips, that'll warm him up. *(He gives Caliban a drink)* Look . . . he's better already. The little glutton even wants some more! Just a second, just a second! *(He walks around the wheelbarrow and sees Trinculo's head sticking out from under the covering)* Jeez! I must be seeing things! A Nindian with two heads! Shit! If I have to pour drink down *two* gullets I won't have much left for myself! Well, never mind. It's incredible . . . your everyday Nindian is already something, but one with two heads . . . a Siamese-twin Nindian, a Nindian with two heads and eight paws, that's really something! My fortune is made. Come on, you wonderful monster, you . . . let's get a look at your other head! *(He draws nearer to Trinculo)* Hello! That face reminds me of something! That nose that shines like a lighthouse . . .

TRINCULO: That gut . . .

STEPHANO: That nose looks familiar . . .

TRINCULO: That gut—there can't be two of them in this lousy world!

STEPHANO: Oh-my-gawd, oh-my-gawd, oh-my-gawd . . . *that's* it . . . it's that crook Trinculo!

TRINCULO: Good lord! It's Stephano!

STEPHANO: So, Trinculo, you were saved too . . . It almost makes you believe God looks after drunks . . .

TRINCULO: Huh! God . . . Bacchus, maybe. As a matter of fact, I reached these welcoming shores by floating on a barrel . . .

STEPHANO: And I by floating on my stomach . . . it's nearly the same thing. But what kind of creature is this? Isn't it a Nindian?

TRINCULO: That's just what I was thinking . . . Yes, by God, it's a Nindian. That's a piece of luck . . . he'll be our guide.

STEPHANO: Judging from the way he can swill it down, he
    doesn't seem to be stupid. I'll try to civilize him. Oh . . .
    not too much, of course. But enough so that he can be
    of some use.

TRINCULO: Civilize him! Shee-it! Does he even know how to
    talk?

STEPHANO: I couldn't get a word out of him, but I know a
    way to loosen his tongue. *(He takes a bottle from his pocket)*

TRINCULO *(Stopping him):* Look here, you're not going to
    waste that nectar on the first savage that comes along,
    are you?

STEPHANO: Selfish! Back off! Let me perform my civilizing
    mission. *(Offering the bottle to Caliban)* Of course, if
    he was cleaned up a bit he'd be worth more to both of
    us. Okay? We'll exploit him together? It's a deal? *(To
    Caliban)* Drink up, pal. You. Drink . . . Yum-yum botty
    botty! *(Caliban drinks)* You, drink more. *(Caliban refuses)*
    You no more thirsty? *(Stephano drinks)* Me always
    thirsty! *(Stephano and Trinculo drink)* Trinculo, you
    know I used to be prejudiced against shipwrecks, but
    I was wrong. They're not bad at all.

TRINCULO: That's true. It seems to make things taste better
    afterwards . . .

STEPHANO: Not to mention the fact that it's got rid of a lot
    of old farts that were always keeping the world down!
    May they rest in peace! But then, you liked them, didn't
    you, all those kings and dukes, all those noblemen! Oh,
    I served them well enough, you've got to earn your
    drink somehow . . . But I could never stand them,
    ever—understand? Never. Trinculo, my friend, I'm a
    long-time believer in the republic . . . you might as well
    say it: I'm a died-in-the-wool believer in the people
    first, a republican in my guts! Down with tyrants!

TRINCULO: Which reminds me . . . If, as it would seem, the
    king and the duke are dead, there's a crown and a
    throne up for grabs around here . . .

STEPHANO: By God, you're right! Smart thinking, Trinculo!
    So, I appoint myself heir . . . I crown myself King of
    the Island.

TRINCULO *(Sarcastically)*: Sure you do! And why you, may
    I ask? I'm the one who thought of it first, that crown!

STEPHANO: Look, Trinculo, don't be silly! I mean, really:
    just take a look at yourself! What's the first thing a king
    needs? Bearing. Presence. And if I've got anything, it's
    that. Which isn't true for everyone. So, I am the king!

CALIBAN: Long live the king!

STEPHANO: It's a miracle . . . he can talk! And what's more,
    he talks sense! O brave savage! *(He embraces Caliban)*
    You see, me dear Trinculo, the people has spoken! Vox
    populi, vox Dei . . . But please, don't be upset.
    Stephano is magnanimous and will never abandon his
    friend Trinculo, the friend who stood by him in his tri-
    als. Trinculo, we've eaten rough bread together, we've
    drunk rot-gut wine together. I want to do something
    for you. I shall appoint you marshal. But we're forget-
    ting our brave savage . . . It's a scientific miracle! He
    can talk!

CALIBAN: Yes, sire. My enthusiasm has restored my speech.
    Long live the king! But beware the usurper!

STEPHANO: Usurper? Who? Trinculo?

CALIBAN: No, the other one . . . Prospero!

STEPHANO: Prospero? Don't know him.

CALIBAN: Well, you see, this island used to belong to me,
    except that a man named Prospero cheated me of it.
    I'm perfectly willing to give you my right to it, but the
    only thing is, you'll have to fight Prospero for it.

STEPHANO: That is of no matter, brave savage. It's a bargain!
   I'll get rid of this Prospero in two shakes.

CALIBAN: Watch out, he's powerful.

STEPHANO: My dear savage, I eat a dozen Prosperos like that
   for breakfast every day. But say no more, say no more!
   Trinculo, take command of the troops! Let us march
   upon the foe!

TRINCULO: Yes, forward march! But first, a drink. We will
   need all our strength and vigor.

CALIBAN: Let's drink, my new-found friends, and let us sing.
   Let us sing of winning the day and of an end to tyranny.
   (Singing:)

> Black pecking creature of the savannas
> the quetzal measures out the new day
> solid and lively
> in its haughty armor.
> Zing! the determined hummingbird
> revels in the flower's depths,
> going crazy, getting drunk,
> a lyrebird gathers up our ravings.
> Freedom hi-day! Freedom hi-day!

STEPHANO AND TRINCULO: Freedom hi-day! Freedom hi-day!

CALIBAN *(Singing)*:

> The ringdove dallies amid the trees,
> wandering the islands, here it rests—
> The white blossoms of the miconia
> mingle with the violet blood of the ripe berries
> and blood stains your plumage,
> traveler!

Lying here after a weary day
we listen to it:
Freedom hi-day! Freedom hi-day!

STEPHANO: Okay, monster . . . enough crooning. Singing
makes a man thirsty. Let's drink instead. Here, have
some more . . . spirits create higher spirits . . . *(Filling
a glass)* Lead the way, O bountiful wine! Soldiers,
forward march! Or rather . . . no: at ease! Night is
falling, the fireflies twinkle, the crickets chirp, all
nature makes its brek-ke-ke-kek! And since night has
fallen, let us take advantage of it to gather our forces
and regain our strength, which has been sorely tried
by the unusually . . . copious emotions of the day. And
tomorrow, at dawn, with a new spring in our step, we'll
have the tyrant's hide. Good night, gentlemen.

(He falls asleep and begins to snore.)

SCENE 3

Prospero's cave.

PROSPERO: So then, Ariel! Where are the gods and goddesses?
They'd better get a move on! And all of them! I want
all of them to take part in the entertainment I have
planned for our dear children. Why do I say "entertainment"? Because starting today I want to inculcate in
them the spectacle of tomorrow's world: logic, beauty,
harmony, the foundations for which I have laid down
by my own willpower. Unfortunately, alas, at my age,

it's time to stop thinking of deeds and to begin thinking of passing on . . . Enter, then!

(Gods and Goddesses enter.)

JUNO: Honor and riches to you! Long continuance and
increasing long life and honored issue! Juno sings to
you her blessings!

CERES: May scarcity and want shun you! That is Ceres'
blessing on you.

IRIS *(Beckoning to the Nymphs)*: Nymphs, come help to cele-
brate here a contract of true love.

(Nymphs enter and dance.)

PROSPERO: My thanks, Goddesses, and my thanks to you,
Iris. Thank you for your good wishes.

(Gods and Goddesses continue their dance.)

FERDINAND: What a splendid and majestic vision! May I be
so bold to think these spirits?

PROSPERO: Yes, spirits which by my art I have from their
confines called to greet you and to bless you.

(Enter Eshu.)

MIRANDA: But who is that? He doesn't look very benevolent!
If I weren't afraid of blaspheming, I'd say he was a
devil rather than a god.

ESHU *(Laughing)*: You are not mistaken, fair lady. God to my
friends, the Devil to my enemies! And lots of laughs
for all!

PROSPERO *(Softly)*: Ariel must have made a mistake. Is my
   magic getting rusty? *(Aloud)* What are you doing here?
   Who invited you? I don't like such loose behavior, even
   from a god!

ESHU: But that's just the point . . . no one invited me . . .
   And that wasn't very nice! Nobody remembered poor
   Eshu! So poor Eshu came anyway. Hihihi! So how
   about something to drink? *(Without waiting for a reply,
   he pours a drink)* . . . Your liquor's not bad. However,
   I must say I prefer dogs! *(Looking at Iris)* I see that
   shocks the little lady, but to each his own. Some prefer
   chickens, others prefer goats. I'm not too fond of
   chickens, myself. But if you're talking about a black
   dog . . . think of poor Eshu!

PROSPERO: Get out! Go away! We will have none of your
   grimaces and buffoonery in this noble assembly. *(He
   makes a magic sign)*

ESHU: I'm going, boss, I'm going . . . But not without a little
   song in honor of the bride and the noble company, as
   you say. *(Singing:)*

> Eshu can play many tricks,
> give him twenty dogs!
> You will see his dirty tricks.
>
> Eshu plays a trick on the queen
> and makes her so upset that she runs
> naked into the street.
>
> Eshu plays a trick on a bride,
> and on the day of the wedding
> she gets into the wrong bed!

Eshu can throw a stone yesterday
and kill a bird today.
He can make a mess out of order and vice-versa.
Ah, Eshu is a wonderful bad joke.
Eshu is not the man to carry a heavy load.
His head comes to a point. When he dances
he doesn't move his shoulders . . .
Oh, Eshu is a merry elf!

Eshu is a merry elf,
and he can whip you with his dick,
he can whip you,
he can whip you . . .

CERES: My dear Iris, don't you find that song quite obscene?
JUNO: It's disgusting! It's quite intolerable . . . if he keeps
on, I'm leaving!
IRIS: It's like Liber, or Priapus!
JUNO: Don't mention that name in my presence!
ESHU *(Continuing to sing)*:

. . . with his dick
he can whip you, whip you . . .

JUNO: Oh! Can't someone get rid of him? I'm not staying
here!
ESHU: Okay, okay . . . Eshu will go. Farewell, my dear col-
leagues! *(Exits)*

(Gods and Goddesses exit.)

PROSPERO: He's gone . . . what a relief! But alas, the harm is
done! I am perturbed . . . My old brain is confused.

Power! Power! Alas! All this will one day fade, like foam, like a cloud, like all the world. And what is power, if I cannot calm my own fears? But come! My power has gone cold. *(Calling)* Ariel!

ARIEL *(Runs in)*: What is it, sire?

PROSPERO: Caliban is alive, he is plotting, he is getting a guerrilla force together and you—you don't say a word! Well, take care of him. Snakes, scorpions, porcupines, all stinging poisonous creatures, he is to be spared nothing! His punishment must be exemplary. Oh, and don't forget the mud and mosquitoes!

ARIEL: Master, let me intercede for him and beg your indulgence. You've got to understand: he's a rebel.

PROSPERO: By his insubordination he's calling into question the whole order of the world. Maybe the Divinity can afford to let him get away with it, but I have a sense of responsibility!

ARIEL: Very well, Master.

PROSPERO: But a thought: arrange some glass trinkets, some trumpery and some second-hand clothes too . . . but colorful ones . . . by the side of the road along which General Caliban and his troops are traveling. Savages adore loud, gaudy clothes . . .

ARIEL: Master . . .

PROSPERO: You're going to make me angry. There's nothing to understand. There is a punishment to be meted out. I will not compromise with evil. Hurry! Unless you want to be the next to feel my wrath.

SCENE 4

In the wild; night is drawing to a close, the murmurings of the spirits of the tropical forest are heard.

VOICE I: Fly!
VOICE II: Here!
VOICE I: Ant!
VOICE II: Here.
VOICE I: Vulture!
VOICE II: Here.
VOICE I: Soft-shelled crab, calao, crab, hummingbird!
VOICES I AND II: Here. Here. Here.
VOICE I: Cramp, crime, fang, opossum!
VOICE II: Kra. Kra. Kra.
VOICE I: Huge hedgehog, you will be our sun today. Shaggy, taloned, stubborn. May it burn! Moon, my fat spider, my big dreamcat, go to sleep, my velvet one.
VOICES I AND II *(Singing)*:

> King-ay
> King-ay
> Von-von
> Maloto
> Vloom-vloom!

(The sun rises. Ariel's band vanishes. Caliban stands for a moment, rubbing his eyes.)

CALIBAN *(Searching the bushes)*: Have to think about getting going again. Away, snakes, scorpions, porcupines! All stinging, biting, sticking beasts! Sting, fever, venom, away! Or if you really want to lick me, do it with a gentle tongue, like the toad whose pure drool soothes me with sweet dreams of the future. For it is for you, for all of us, that I go forth today to face the common enemy. Yes, hereditary and common. Look, a hedgehog! Sweet little thing . . . How can any animal—any natural animal, if I may put it that way—go against me on the day I'm setting forth to conquer Prospero! Unimaginable! Prospero is the Anti-Nature! And I say, down with Anti-Nature! And does the porcupine bristle his spines at that? No, he smoothes them down! That's nature! It's kind and gentle, in a word. You've just got to know how to deal with it. So come on, the way is clear! Off we go!

(The band sets out. Caliban marches forward singing his battle song:)

Shango carries a big stick,
he strikes and money expires!
He strikes and lies expire!
He strikes and larceny expires!
Shango, Shango ho!

Shango is the gatherer of the rain,
he passes, wrapped in his fiery cloak,
his horse's hoofs strike lighting
on the pavements of the sky!
Shango is a great knight!
Shango, Shango ho!

*(The roar of the sea can be heard.
Enter Stephano and Trinculo.)*

STEPHANO: Tell me, brave savage, what is that noise? It
     sounds like the roaring of a beast at bay.

CALIBAN: Not at bay . . . more like on the prowl . . . Don't
     worry, it's a pal of mine.

STEPHANO: You are very close-mouthed about the company
     you keep.

CALIBAN: And yet it helps me breathe. That's why I call it a
     pal. Sometimes it sneezes, and a drop falls on my fore-
     head and cools me with its salt, or blesses me . . .

STEPHANO: I don't understand. You aren't drunk, are you?

CALIBAN: Come on! It's that howling impatient thing that
     suddenly appears in a clap of thunder like some god
     and hits you in the face, that rises up out of the very
     depths of the abyss and smites you with its fury! It's
     the sea!

STEPHANO: Odd country! And an odd baptism!

CALIBAN: But the best is still the wind and the songs it sings
     . . . its dirty sigh when it rustles through the bushes, or
     its triumphant chant when it passes by breaking trees,
     remnants of their terror in its beard.

STEPHANO: The savage is delirious, he's raving mad! Tough
     luck, Trinculo, our savage is playing without a full deck!

TRINCULO: I'm kind of shuffling myself . . . In other words,
     I'm exhausted. I never knew such hard going! Savage,
     even your mud is muddier.

CALIBAN: That isn't mud . . . it's something Prospero's
     dreamed up.

TRINCULO: There's a savage for you . . . everything's always
     caused by someone. The sun is Prospero's smile. The
     rain is the tear in Prospero's eye . . . And I suppose the
     mud is Prospero's shit. And what about the mosqui-
     toes? What are they, may I ask? Zzzzzz, Zzzzzz . . . do
     you hear them? My face is being eaten off!

CALIBAN: Those aren't mosquitoes. Its some kind of gas that stings your nose and throat and makes you itch. It's another of Prospero's tricks. It's part of his arsenal.

STEPHANO: What do you mean by that?

CALIBAN: I mean his anti-riot arsenal! He's got a lot of gadgets like these . . . gadgets to make you deaf, to blind you, to make you sneeze, to make you cry . . .

TRINCULO: And to make you slip! Shit! This is some fix you've got us in! I can't take anymore . . . I'm going to sit down!

STEPHANO: Come on, Trinculo, show a little courage! We're engaged in a mobile ground maneuver here, and you know what that means: drive, initiatives, split-second decisions to meet new eventualities, and—above all—mobility. Let's go! Up you get! Mobility!

TRINCULO: But my feet are bleeding!

STEPHANO: Get up or I'll knock you down! *(Trinculo begins to walk again)* But tell me, my good savage, this usurper of yours seems very well protected. It might be dangerous to attack him!

CALIBAN: You mustn't underestimate him. You mustn't overestimate him, either . . . he's showing his power, but he's doing it mostly to impress us.

STEPHANO: No matter. Trinculo, we must take precautions. Axiom: never underestimate the enemy. Here, pass me that bottle. I can always use it as a club.

(Highly colored clothing is seen, hanging from a rope.)

TRINCULO: Right, Stephano. On with the battle. Victory means loot. And there's a foretaste of it . . . look at that fine wardrobe! Trinculo, my friend, methinks you are going to put on those britches . . . they'll replace your torn trousers.

STEPHANO: Look out, Trinculo . . . one move and I'll knock you down. As your lord and master I have the first pick, and with those britches I'm exercising my feudal rights . . .

TRINCULO: I saw them first!

STEPHANO: The king gets first pick in every country in the world.

TRINCULO: That's tyranny, Stephano. I'm not going to let you get away with it.

(They fight.)

CALIBAN: Let it alone, fool. I tell you about winning your dignity, and you start fighting over hand-me-downs! *(To himself)* To think I'm stuck with these jokers! What an idiot I am! How could I ever have thought I could create the Revolution with swollen guts and fat faces! Oh well! History won't blame me for not having been able to win my freedom all by myself.

It's you and me, Prospero! *(Weapon in hand, he advances on Prospero, who has just appeared)*

PROSPERO *(Bares his chest to him)*: Strike! Go on, strike! Strike your master, your benefactor! Don't tell me you're going to spare him!

(Caliban raises his arm, but hesitates.)

Go on! You don't dare! See, you're nothing but an animal . . . you don't know how to kill.

CALIBAN: Defend yourself! I'm not a murderer.

PROSPERO *(Very calm)*: The worse for you. You've lost your
       chance. Stupid as a slave! And now, enough of this
       farce. *(Calling)* Ariel!

(Enter Ariel.)

Ariel, take charge of the prisoners!

(Caliban, Trinculo and Stephano are taken prisoners.)

SCENE 5

Prospero's cave. Miranda and Ferdinand are playing chess.

MIRANDA: Sir, I think you're cheating
FERDINAND: And what if I told you that I would not do so
       for twenty kingdoms?
MIRANDA: I would not believe a word of it, but I would
       forgive you. Now, be honest . . . you did cheat!
FERDINAND: I'm pleased that you were able to tell.
       (Laughing) That makes me less worried at the thought
       that soon you will be leaving your innocent flowery
       kingdom for my less-innocent world of men.
MIRANDA: Oh, you know that, hitched to your star, I would
       brave the demons of hell!

(The Nobles enter.)

ALONSO: My son! This marriage! The thrill of it has struck
       me dumb! The thrill and the joy!

GONZALO: A happy ending to a most opportune shipwreck!

ALONSO: A unique one, indeed, for it can legitimately be described as such.

GONZALO: Look at them! Isn't it wonderful! I've been too choked up to speak, or I would have already told these children all the joy my old heart feels at seeing them living love's young dream and cherishing each other so tenderly.

ALONSO *(To Ferdinand and Miranda)*: My children, give me your hands. May the Lord bless you.

GONZALO: Amen! Amen!

(Enter Prospero.)

PROSPERO: Thank you, gentlemen, for having agreed to join in this little family party. Your presence has brought us comfort and joy. However, you must now think of getting some rest. Tomorrow morning, you will recover your vessels—they are undamaged—and your men, who I can guarantee are safe, hale and hearty. I shall return with you to Europe, and I can promise you—I should say: promise us—a rapid sail and propitious winds.

GONZALO: God be praised! We are delighted . . . delighted and overcome! What a happy, what a memorable day! With one voyage Antonio has found a brother, his brother has found a dukedom, his daughter has found a husband. Alonso has regained his son and gained a daughter. And what else? . . . Anyway, I am the only one whose emotion prevents him from knowing what he's saying . . .

PROSPERO: The proof of that, my fine Gonzalo, is that you are forgetting someone: Ariel, my loyal servant.

(Turning to Ariel) Yes, Ariel, today you will be free.
Go, my sweet. I hope you will not be bored.

ARIEL: Bored! I fear that the days will seem all too short!

> There, where the Cecropia gloves its impatient
>   hands with
> silver,
> where the ferns free the stubborn black stumps
> from their scored bodies with a green cry—
> There where the intoxicating berry ripens at the visit
> of the wild ring-dove
> through the throat of that musical bird
> I shall let fall
> one by one,
> each more pleasing than the last
> four notes so sweet that the last
> will give rise to a yearning
> in the heart of the most forgetful slaves
> yearning for freedom!

PROSPERO: Come, come. All the same, you are not going to
set my world on fire with your music, I trust!

ARIEL *(With intoxication)*:

> Or on some stony plane
> perched on an agave stalk
> I shall be the thrush that launches
> its mocking cry
> to the benighted field-hand,
> "Dig, nigger! Dig, nigger!"
> and the lightened agave will
> straighten from my flight,
> a solemn flag.

PROSPERO: That is a very unsettling agenda! Go! Scram!
Before I change my mind!

(Enter Stephano, Trinculo, Caliban.)

GONZALO: Sire, here are your people.

PROSPERO: Oh no, not all of them! Some are yours.

ALONSO: True. There's that fool Trinculo and that unspeakable Stephano.

STEPHANO: The very ones, sire, in person. We throw ourselves at your merciful feet.

ALONSO: What became of you?

STEPHANO: Sire, we were walking through the forest—no, it was in the fields—when we saw some perfectly respectable clothing blowing in the wind. We thought it only right to collect them and we were returning them to their rightful owner when a frightful adventure befell us . . .

TRINCULO: Yes, we were mistaken for thieves and treated accordingly.

STEPHANO: Yes, sire, it is the most dreadful thing that could happen to an honest man: victims of a judicial error, a miscarriage of justice!

PROSPERO: Enough! Today is a day to be benevolent, and it will do no good to try and talk sense to you in the state you're in . . . Leave us. Go sleep it off, drunkards. We raise sail tomorrow.

TRINCULO: Raise sail! But that's what we do all the time, sire, Stephano and I . . . at least, we raise our glasses, from dawn till dusk till dawn. The hard part is putting them down, landing, as you might say.

PROSPERO: Scoundrels! If only life could bring you to the safe harbors of Temperance and Sobriety!

ALONSO *(Indicating Caliban)*: That is the strangest creature
    I've ever seen!

PROSPERO: And the most devilish too!

GONZALO: What's that? Devilish! You've reprimanded him,
    preached at him, you've ordered and made him obey
    and you say he is still indomitable!

PROSPERO: Honest Gonzalo, it is as I have said.

GONZALO: Well—and forgive me, counselor, if I give coun-
    sel—on the basis of my long experience the only thing
    left is exorcism. "Begone, unclean spirit, in the name of
    the Father, of the Son and of the Holy Ghost." That's
    all there is to it!

(Caliban bursts out laughing.)

    You were absolutely right! And more so than you
    thought . . . He's not just a rebel, he's a real tough
    customer! *(To Caliban)* So much the worse for you, my
    friend. I have tried to save you. I give up. I leave you to
    the secular arm!

PROSPERO: Come here, Caliban. Have you got anything to
    say in your own defense? Take advantage of my good
    humor. I'm in a forgiving mood today.

CALIBAN: I'm not interested in defending myself. My only
    regret is that I've failed.

PROSPERO: What were you hoping for?

CALIBAN: To get back my island and regain my freedom.

PROSPERO: And what would you do all alone here on this
    island, haunted by the devil, tempest tossed?

CALIBAN: First of all, I'd get rid of you! I'd spit you out, all
    your works and pomps! Your "white" magic!

PROSPERO: That's a fairly negative program . . .

CALIBAN: You don't understand it . . . I say I'm going to spit you out, and that's very positive . . .

PROSPERO: Well, the world is really upside down . . . We've seen everything now: Caliban as a dialectician! However, in spite of everything I'm fond of you, Caliban. Come, let's make peace. We've lived together for ten years and worked side by side! Ten years count for something after all! We've ended up by becoming compatriots!

CALIBAN: You know very well that I'm not interested in peace. I'm interested in being free! Free, you hear?

PROSPERO: It's odd . . . no matter what you do, you won't succeed in making me believe that I'm a tyrant!

CALIBAN: Understand what I say, Prospero:

> For years I bowed my head
> for years I took it, all of it—
> your insults, your ingratitude . . .
> and worst of all, more degrading than all the rest,
> your condescension.
> But now, it's over!
> Over, do you hear?
> Of course, at the moment
> you're still stronger than I am.
> But I don't give a damn for your power
> or for your dogs or your police or your inventions!
> And do you know why?
> It's because I know I'll get you.
> I'll impale you! And on a stake that you've
>   sharpened yourself!
> You'll have impaled yourself!
> Prospero, you're a great magician:
> you're an old hand at deception.

And you lied to me so much,
about the world, about myself,
that you ended up by imposing on me
an image of myself:
underdeveloped, in your words, undercompetent
that's how you made me see myself!
And I hate that image . . . and it's false!
But now I know you, you old cancer,
And I also know myself!
And I know that one day
my bare fist, just that,
will be enough to crush your world!
The old world is crumbling down!

Isn't it true? Just look!
It even bores you to death.
And by the way . . . you have a chance to get it over
    with:
you can pick up and leave.
You can go back to Europe.
But the hell you will!
I'm sure you won't leave.
You make me laugh with your "mission"!
Your "vocation"!
Your vocation is to hassle me.
And that's why you'll stay,
just like those guys who founded the colonies
and who now can't live anywhere else.
You're just an old addict, that's what you are!

PROSPERO: Poor Caliban! You know that you're headed
    towards your own ruin. You're sliding towards suicide!

You know I will be the stronger, and stronger all the
time. I pity you!

CALIBAN: And I hate you!

PROSPERO: Beware! My generosity has its limits.

CALIBAN *(Shouting)*:

> Shango marches with strength
> along his path, the sky!
> Shango is a fire-bearer,
> his steps shake the heavens
> and the earth
> Shango, Shango, ho!

PROSPERO:

> I have uprooted the oak and raised the sea,
> I have caused the mountain to tremble
> and have bared my chest to adversity.
> With Jove I have traded thunderbolt for thunderbolt.
> Better yet—from a brutish monster I have made
>   man!
> But ah! To have failed to find the path to man's
>   heart ...
> if that be where man is.

(To Caliban:)

> Well, I hate you as well!
> For it is you who have made me
> doubt myself for the first time.

(To the Nobles:)

... My friends, come near. We must say farewell ... I shall not be going with you. My fate is here: I shall not run from it.

ANTONIO: What, sire?

PROSPERO: Hear me well:

> I am not in any ordinary sense a master,
> as this savage thinks,
> but rather the conductor of a boundless score:
> this isle,
> summoning voices, I alone,
> and mingling them at my pleasure,
> arranging out of confusion
> one intelligible line.

Without me, who would be able to draw music from all that?

> This isle is mute without me.
> My duty, thus, is here,
> and here I shall stay.

GONZALO: Oh day full rich in miracles!

PROSPERO: Do not be distressed. Antonio, be you the lieutenant of my goods and make use of them as procurator until that time when Ferdinand and Miranda may take effective possession of them, joining them with the Kingdom of Naples. Nothing of that which has been set for them must be postponed: let their marriage be celebrated at Naples with all royal splendor. Honest Gonzalo, I place my trust in your word. You shall stand as father to our princess at this ceremony.

GONZALO: Count on me, sire.

PROSPERO: Gentlemen, farewell.

(Exit all but Prospero and Caliban.)

> And now, Caliban, it's you and me!
> What I have to tell you will be brief:
> ten times, a hundred times, I've tried to save you,
> above all from yourself.
> But you have always answered me with wrath
> and venom,
> like the opossum that pulls itself up by its own tail
> the better to bite the hand that tears it from the
>   darkness.
> Well, my boy, I shall set aside my indulgent nature
> And henceforth I will answer your violence
> with violence!

(Time passes, symbolized by the curtain's being lowered halfway and reraised. In semi-darkness Prospero appears, aged and weary. His gestures are jerky and automatic, his speech weak, toneless, trite.)

Odd, but for some time now we seem to be overrun with opossums. They're everywhere. Peccarys, wild boar, all this unclean nature! But mainly opossums. Those eyes! The vile grins they have! It's as though the jungle was laying siege to the cave . . . But I shall stand firm . . . I shall not let my work perish! *(Shouting)* I shall protect civilization! *(He fires in all directions)* They're done for! Now, this way I'll be able to have some peace and quiet for a while. But it's cold. Odd how the climate's changed. Cold on this island . . . Have to think about making a fire . . . Well, Caliban,

old fellow, it's just us two now, here on the island . . .
only you and me. You and me. You-me . . . me-you!
What in the hell is he up to? *(Shouting)* Caliban!

*(In the distance, above the sound of the surf and the chirp-
ing of birds, we hear snatches of Caliban's song:)*

CALIBAN:

FREEDOM HI-DAY! FREEDOM HI-DAY!

END OF PLAY

Annex

LITERAL TRANSLATIONS OF SONGS

ARIEL'S SONG (ACT I, SCENE 2)

Chestnut horse of the sand
they bite out the place
where the waves expire in
pure languor.
When the waves die
here come all,
join hands
and dance.

Blond sands,
what fire!
Languorous waves,
pure expiration.

Here lips lick and lick again
our wounds.

The waves make a waterline . . .
Nothing is, all is becoming . . .
The season is close and strange.

The eye is a fine pearl
the heart of coral, the bone of coral,
there, at the waterline
as the sea swells within us.

TRINCULO'S SONG (ACT III, SCENE 2)

Virginia, with tears in my eyes
I bid you farewell.
We're off to Mexico,
straight into the setting sun.

With sails unfurled, my dear love,
it torments me to leave you,
a tempest is brewing
some storm is howling
that will carry off the entire crew!

STEPHANO'S SONG (ACT III, SCENE 2)

(Obviously an old sea chantey or Césaire's adaptation of one)

Bravely on, guys, step it lively,
bravely on, farewell Bordeaux,

to Cape Horn, it won't be hot,
off to hunt the whale.

More than one of us will lose his skin
farewell misery, farewell ship.
The ones who return with all flags flying
will be the first-rate sailors . . .

AIMÉ CÉSAIRE was born in Martinique in 1913. He is a world-renowned poet, essayist and dramatist. He was the founding editor of *Tropiques*, which was instrumental in establishing the use of surrealism as a political weapon. He is the author of six books of poetry since the landmark volume *Cahier d'un retour au pays natal* (*Notebook of a Return to My Native Land*) published in 1939. His first play, *Et les chiens se taisaient* (*And the Dogs Were Silent*, 1956) was directed by Gabriel Garran at the Théâtre de la Commune d'Aubervilliers. His three subsequent plays—*La Tragédie du roi Christophe* (*The Tragedy of King Christophe*, 1963), *Une Saison au Congo* (*A Season in the Congo*, 1967) and *Une Tempête* (1969)—were first directed by the late Jean-Marie Serreau. They have often been revived, and *La Tragédie du roi Christophe* is now part of the repertory of the Comédie-Française. *Une Tempête* has been produced in France, the Middle East, Africa and the West Indies. It had its American premiere in Richard Miller's translation at Ubu Repertory Theater, in 1991. *A Season in the Congo*, translated by Ralph Manheim, is included in *Theater and Politics: An International Anthology*, published by Ubu Repertory Theater Publications, 1990. Césaire has held a number of government positions in his native Martinique, including that of Mayor of Fort-de-France.

RICHARD MILLER has translated many books, both nonfiction and fiction, including works by Roland Barthes, Brassaï and Albert Camus, as well as poetry, many articles and a number of plays. Among his more recent translations are *Scent* by Annick Le Guérer and *Beethoven's Ninth* by Esteban Buch, which will be published in late 2002. He lives in Paris.